INTRODUCTION TO ART SONG

SOPRANO

Songs in English for
Classical Voice Students

Compiled by Joan Frey Boytim

ISBN 978-1-4950-6464-7

To access companion recorded piano accompaniments online, visit:
www.halleonard.com/mylibrary

Enter Code
4641-3098-3382-7841

G. SCHIRMER, *Inc.*

7777 W. BLUEMOUND RD. P.O. BOX 13819 MILWAUKEE, WI 53213

www.musicsalesclassical.com
www.halleonard.com

PREFACE

Introduction to Art Song is intended for any beginning classical singer, teenager through adult. In most studios we have students who remain in traditional voice lessons for any number of years. As teachers, this gives us the time to determine the work ethic, the innate talent, and the personality of the student as we explore repertoire. In addition, we often accept beginning students who, for a number of reasons, will only be in our studios for a year or less. It seemed desirable to develop a book of previously successful, well-liked songs in English which are not particularly difficult, yet more mature than the *Easy Songs for Beginning Singers* series for use with these students.

A teacher browsing through the collections will find many familiar songs, but often in alternate keys from what has been previously published. Very often after recitals students will ask to sing a song they heard another singer perform from *The First Book of Solos* series, but it is not published in a suitable key. Some male voice examples: "When I Think Upon the Maidens," "Brother Will, Brother John," "Give a Man a Horse He Can Ride" and "Shenandoah." Female voice examples are "I Love All Graceful Things," "Danny Boy," "The Green Dog," and "Come to the Fair." In my own teaching some of my students will want to have their voice type appropriate volume of *Introduction to Art Song* for access to songs in comfortable keys.

Songs from American and British composers appear which are not included in previous collections. Of special interest are three, short, early songs by Samuel Barber only recently published: "Longing," "Thy Love" and "Music, When Soft Voices Die."

No sacred songs, Christmas songs or spirituals have been included, which makes the collections practical for use in beginning voice classes. The vocal ranges are moderate and the accompaniments are not extremely difficult. Each volume includes 15 to 20 songs.

This final set of four anthologies completes my various compilations of vocal repertoire books for beginning to intermediate singers, which began in 1991 with *The First Book of Solos*.

I want to thank my inspiring editor, Richard Walters, for believing in me, and offering his fine guidance, patience, friendship, and promoting the 60 published compilations, which I hope have made life easier for teachers all over the world. I also wish to thank Hal Leonard Corporation for giving me this amazing opportunity.

Joan Frey Boytim
compiler

CONTENTS

Pianists on the recordings: [1]Laura Ward, [2]Brendan Fox

The price of this publication includes access to companion recorded accompaniments online, for download or streaming, using the unique code found on the title page. Visit www.**halleonard.com/mylibrary** and enter the access code.

to Helen-Claire Moyle

AMERICAN LULLABY

Gladys Rich

14
win-dow shade high,
So you can see the cars whiz-zing by.
17
poco accel.
f
a tempo
mp
Home in a hur - ry each Dad-dy must fly To a ba - by like
poco accel.
f
a tempo
mf
3
20
you.
mp
Hush - a - bye, you sweet lit-tle ba - by, And
p
24
close those pret - ty blue eyes.
Moth-er has gone to her

27
week-ly bridge par - ty To get her wee ba - by the prize.
3
30
mf
Nurs-ie will turn the ra-di-o on,
mf
33
So you can hear a sleep-y-time song,
Sung by a la - dy whose
36
rall.
mf
a tempo
mp
dim. e rall.
poor heart must long For a ba - by like you!
3
l.h.
mf
rall.
a tempo
dim. e rall.

THE BLUE-BELL

from *From an Old Garden*

Margaret Deland

Edward MacDowell
Op. 26, No. 5

9
give your heart to me!"
ten. in time
pp leggieriss.
12
ppp legatiss.
una corda
14
pp
"I love but you,
17
poco rall.
And I'll be true,
poco rall.
dolciss.

19
p
rall.
Oh, give me your heart, your heart, I
pp
rall.
22
pp very slowly
yet slower
f fast
pray!" She bent her head, "I will!" she said, When
very slowly
yet slower
pp
ppp
25
ff
lo!
fast
ten.
fz
ff
ten.
27
ff
fast
he flew a - way.
8va
fz
ff
r.h.
l.h.

CLOUD-SHADOWS

from *Three Songs*

Katharine Pyle

James H. Rogers

14
a tempo
mp con anima
pp
still. O - ver the dai - sy field they passed, And
a tempo
mp
pp
17
mf
slargando
not a dai - sy stirr'd; They moved like char - i - ots
slargando
mf poco marcato
20
p
a tempo
grand and slow, But nev - er a sound was heard.
p
a tempo
23
p
I

27
molto tranquillo
wish I could ride on the shad - ows of clouds, Could ride till, the jour - ney
ten.
ten.
30
più lento
molto rall.
done, I'd find my - self at the end of the world, Where the
più lento
ten.
ten.
molto rall.
33
a tempo
earth and the sky are one.
pp
dolciss.
a tempo
sempre tranquillo
37
rall.
molto rall.
pp
rall.
dim.
molto rall.

LONGING

from *Two Poems of the Wind*

Fiona Macleod (William Sharp)

Samuel Barber

12
thee. In the dew on the grass is your name, dear, i' the
15
very softly
leaf on the tree— O would I were the
pp
18
Much slower
cool wind that's blow - ing from the sea. O
21
would I were the cool wind that's blow - ing far from

*The optional note appears in Barber's manuscript.

BENEATH A WEEPING WILLOW'S SHADE

Francis Hopkinson
arranged by Harold Milligan

poco rit.
wil - low's shade, She sat and sang a - lone; Her
strains re - plied, The winds her sor - rows bore; "A -
poco rit.
mf
a tempo
poco rit.
hand up - on her heart she laid, And plain - tive was her
dieu dear youth, A - dieu! she cried, "I ne'er shall see thee
a tempo
poco rit.
p a tempo
moan, And plain - tive was her moan.
more, I ne'er shall see thee more."
The
p a tempo
mock - bird sat up - on a bough,
tr
quasi ad lib.

26
molto rit.
a tempo
The mock - bird sat up - on a bough, And
molto rit.
a tempo
tr
29
mf
lis - ten'd to her lay Then to the dis - tant
mf
32
hills he bore the dul - cet notes a - way Then
35
to the dis - tant hills he bore The dul - cet notes a -

38
way the dul - cet notes a - way the
41
dul - cet notes a - way
1.
tr
quasi ad lib.
44
rit.
a tempo
Fond
47
2.
way.

COME BACK!

from *Two Songs*

Roger Quilter

11
f passionately
glow with love and light di - vine; "Come
cresc.
13
quicker
back! come back! my love," I cried. "Come
f
quicker
15
ff
back, come back, my love, my
ff
17
life!
ff
sff

CORALS

Zoë Akins

Bryceson Treharne

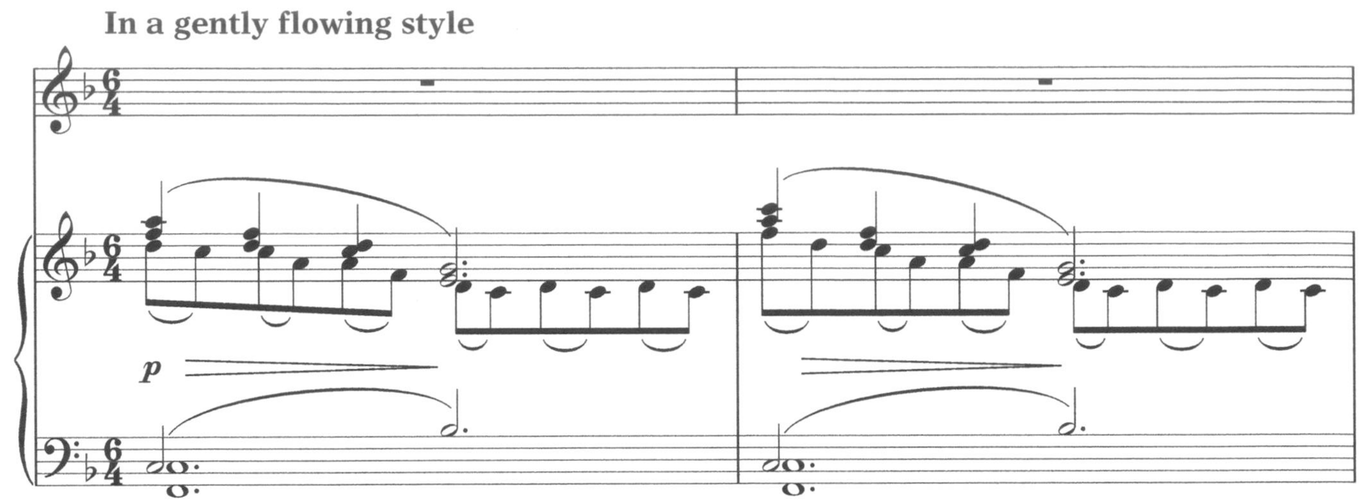

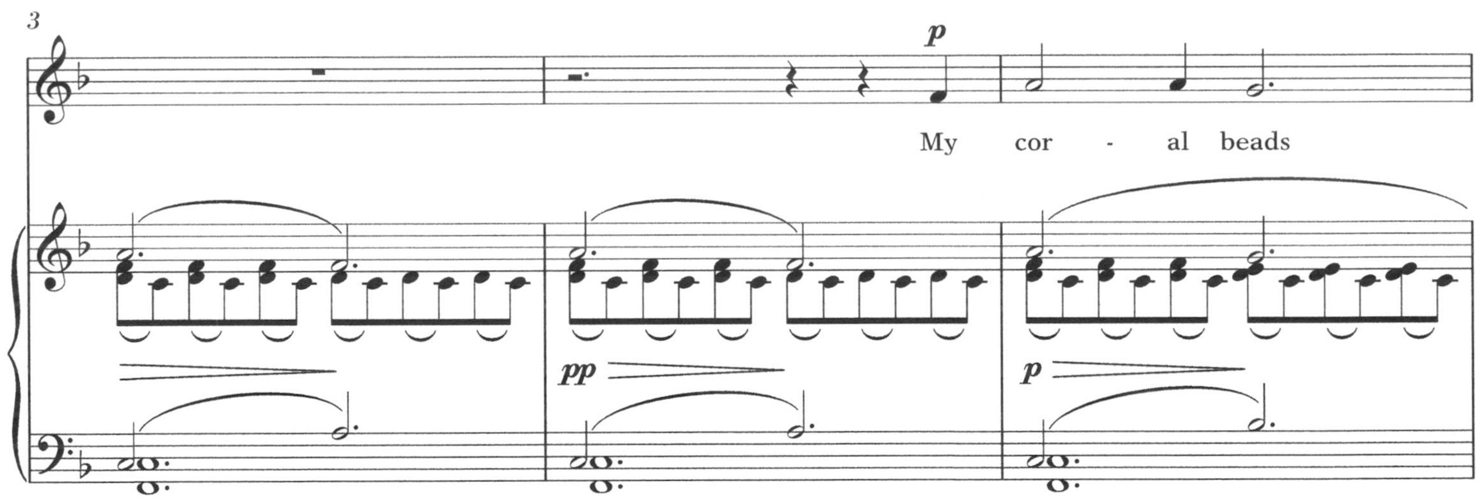

9
poco rit.
a tempo
It was a young mer - maid who gave This strand of rose to
poco rit.
a tempo
12
mp
me. She has a cas - tle
p
15
like a shell Of o - pal - col - oured hue;
18
poco rit.
ten.
She has a sweet - toned gold - en bell That rings the whole night
mp
poco rit.
colla voce

21
a tempo
mf
through. Her hair is long, her
mf a tempo
24
ten.
opt.
eyes are deep And sap - phire like the waves;
colla voce
Poco lento
27
a tempo
She has no grief to make her weep, And gold - fish are her
mf
p a tempo
30
poco rit.
a tempo
slaves, and gold - fish are her slaves. And
poco rit.
colla voce
a tempo

33
in her cas - tle she can lie With sea - flow'rs in her
pp
36
hands, And hear the murmur go - ing by Of
39
ships to oth - er lands, to oth - er
p dim.
p
42
lands.
pp dim.
ppp

DANNY BOY

Fred E. Weatherly

Old Irish Air

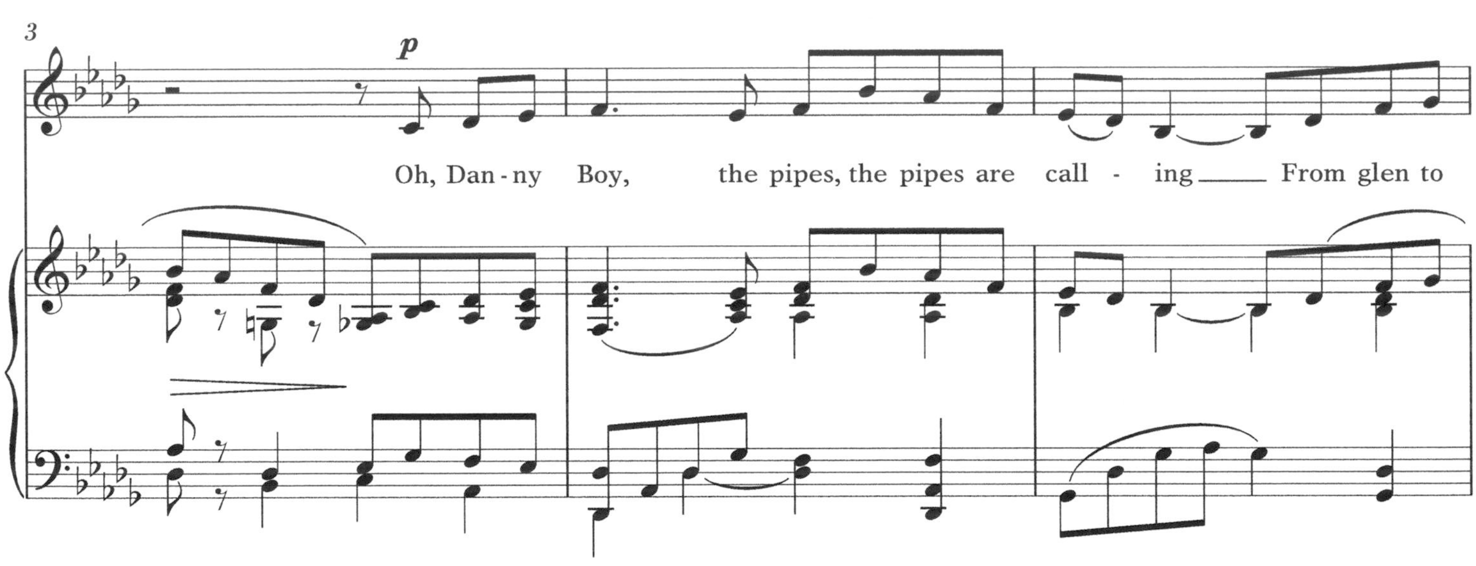

8
gone, and all the ros - es fall - ing, It's you, it's you must go, and I must
11
bide. But come ye back when sum - mer's in the mea - dow, Or when the
mf
14
val - ley's hushed and white with snow, It's I'll be here in sun - shine or in
17
sha - dow, Oh, Dan - ny Boy, oh, Dan - ny Boy, I love you so!

20
p
but when ye come, and all the flow'rs are
cresc.
sempre legato
dolce
23
dy - ing, If I am dead, as dead I well may
espress.
25
be, Ye'll come and find the place where I am
27
ly - ing, And kneel and say an A - ve there for me; And I shall
pp
pp

30
hear, though soft you tread a - bove me, And all my
32
grave will warm - er, sweet - er be, For you will
34
sempre pp
bend and tell me that you love me, And I shall
poco rit.
sempre pp
poco cresc. e rit.
36
più lento.
rall.
sleep in peace un - til you come to me!
più lento.
rall.
ppp

to my friend, Florence Koehler

DREAM VALLEY

from *Three Songs of William Blake*

William Blake

Roger Quilter
Op. 20, No. 1

14
drink of the clear stream, And hear the lin-net's song, And there I'll lie and dream The
pp
una corda
p
17
mp poco più sonoro
day a-long; And, when night comes, I'll go To plac-es fit for woe,
mp tre corde
20
p
poco rit.
Walk-ing a-long the dark-en'd val-ley With si-lent Mel-an-chol-y
dolce
p
poco rit.
23
rit.
espress.
poco rit.
a tempo ma tranquillo
pp una corda
pp
rit.

GO 'WAY FROM MY WINDOW

John Jacob Niles

7
both - er me on more.
long as song - birds sing.
on ac - count of you.
real - ly did love best.
I'll
I'll
Go
Go 'way from my win - dow, Go
10
'way from my door, Go 'way, 'way, 'way from my bed - side And
3
mf
12
rit. e dim.
both - er me no more, And both - er me no more.
rit. e dim.

THE LASS FROM THE LOW COUNTREE

John Jacob Niles

11
mp
sor - row! Now she sleeps in the val - ley where the wild - flow-ers nod, And
mp
14
dim.
p
no one knows she loved him but her - self and God. One
dim.
p
17
mf
morn, when the sun was on the mead, He passed by her door on a
mf
8
8
8

20
p
milk-white steed; She smil - ed and she spoke, but he paid no heed. Oh,
p
23
mp
sor - row, sing sor - row! Now she sleeps in the val - ley where the
mp
26
dim.
p
wild - flow - ers nod, And no one knows she loved him but her - self and God.
dim.
p
29
mp
If you be a lass from the Low Coun-tree, Don't
mp

32
mf
f
love of no lord of ___ high de-gree; They hain't got a heart for
35
p
mp
sym - pa - thy. Oh, sor - row, sing sor - row! Now she
38
sleeps in the val - ley where the wild - flow - ers nod. And
40
dim.
p
no one knows she loved him but her - self and God.
pp

MUSIC, WHEN SOFT VOICES DIE

Percy Bysshe Shelley

Samuel Barber

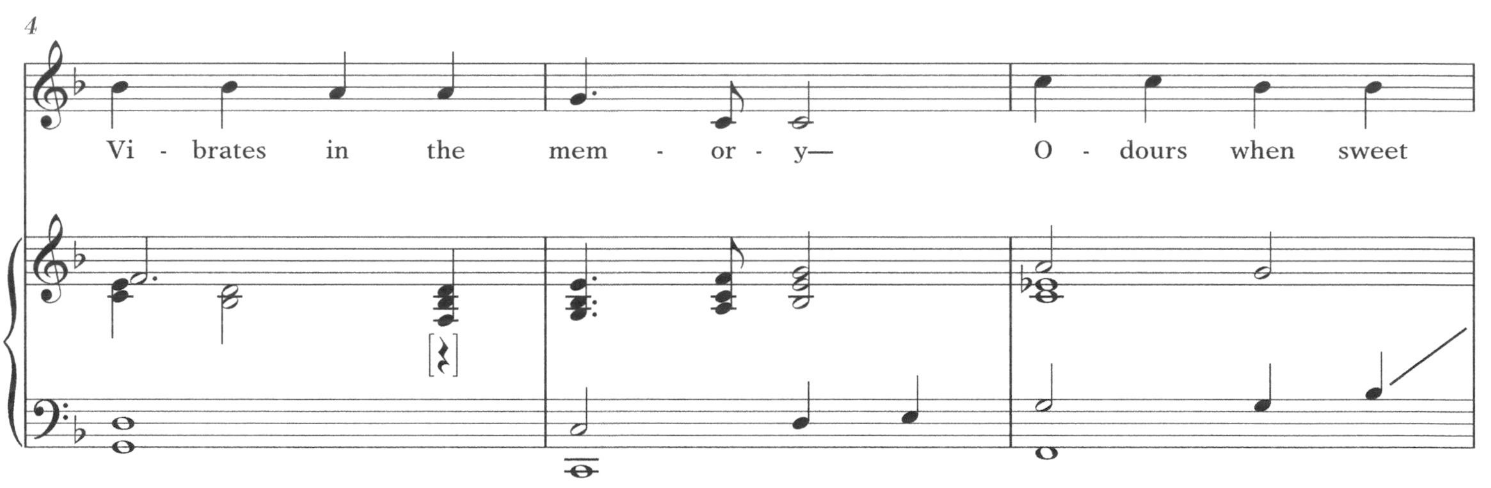

10
Rose leaves, when the rose is dead, Are heap'd for the be -

13
lov - ed's bed; And so thy thoughts when thou are gone,

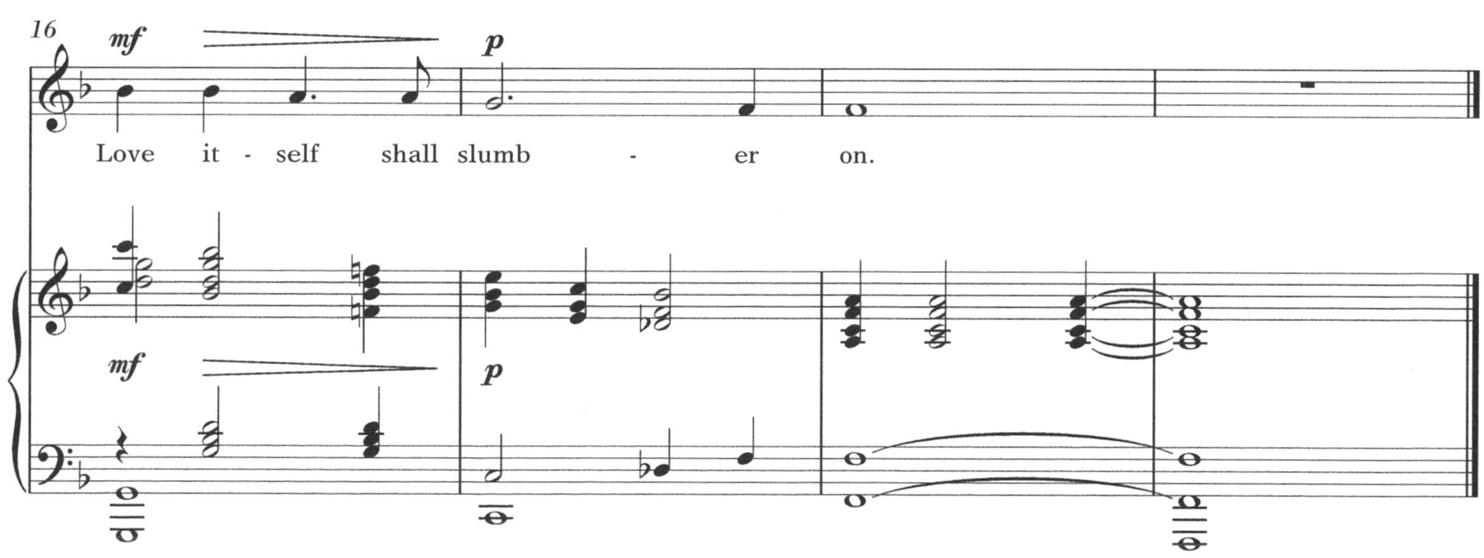
16
Love it - self shall slumb - er on.

MY LOVER IS A FISHERMAN

Lily Strickland

11
f
mf
out with the dawn each morn - ing. With his nets so strong Stays he
f
14
poco rit.
animato
all the day long, And many - y are the fish he gath - ers. Oh, my
mf
poco rit.
animato
17
f
lov - er is a fish - er - man, And he sails on the big blue
f
20
p tenderly
riv - er. Soon he'll come for me in the e - ven - tide, In his
l.h.
dolce
grazioso

23
rall.
espress.
lit - tle boat with the crim - son sails; And I'll sail a - way down the
espress.
rall.
26
mf
ten.
sost.
big blue riv - er, With my lov - er, Mine for
mf
28
a tempo primo
ev - er, Oh, my lov - er is a
6
a tempo primo
6
30
f
fish - er - man, And he'll come for me ver - y soon!

THE SKY ABOVE THE ROOF

Mable Dearmer
from the French of Paul Verlaine

Ralph Vaughan Williams

13
bell from out the blue Drow - si - ly rings: A
pp
16
bird from out the blue Plain - tive - ly sings.
3
19
mf più lento
Ah God! a life is here, Sim - ple and fair,
mf
22
Mur - murs of strife are here Lost in the

25
mf
air.
Why dost thou
p
mf
29
weep, O heart, Poured out in tears?
What hast thou
33
f
pp
done, O heart, ___ With thy spent _ years?
f
pp
36
Più lento
pp
ppp

SLUMBER SONG

from *Five Songs*

English version by
Charles Fonteyn Manney

Alexander Gretchaninoff
Op. 1, No. 5

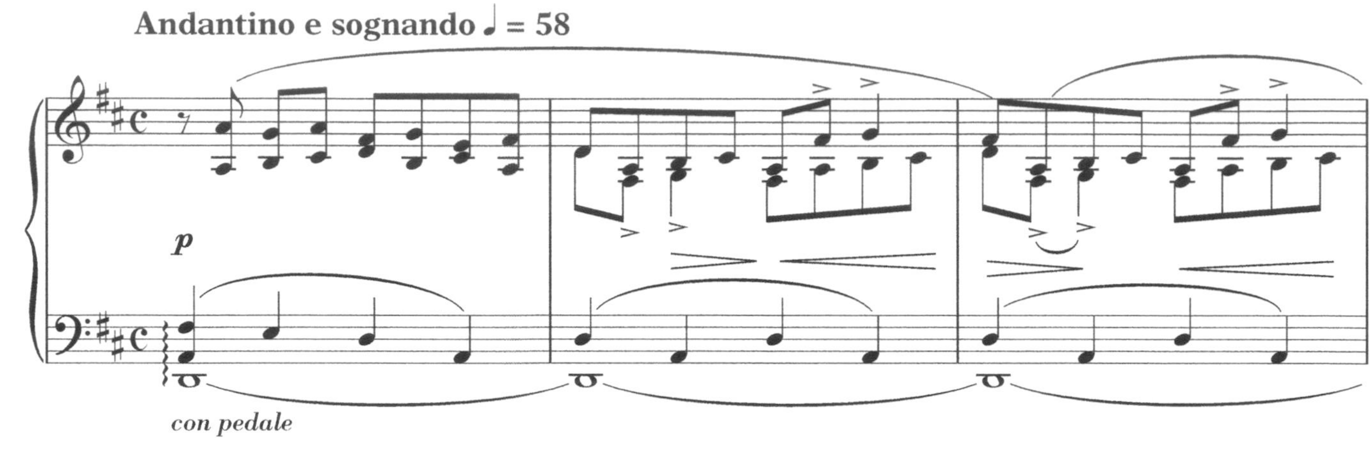

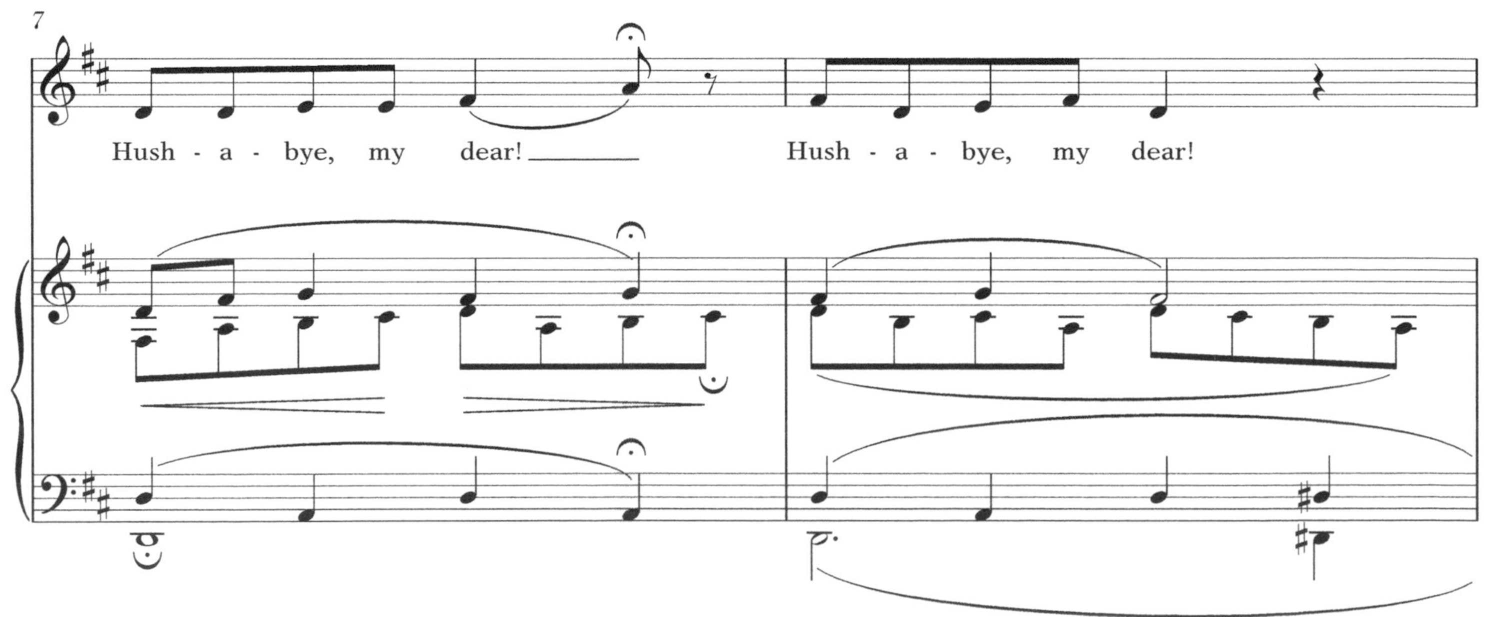

9
While I rock your little cradle
11
rit.
p a tempo
In the moon - light clear.
Songs I sing and
cantabile
rit.
p a tempo
14
ten.
tales I tell you, That you love to hear;
mp

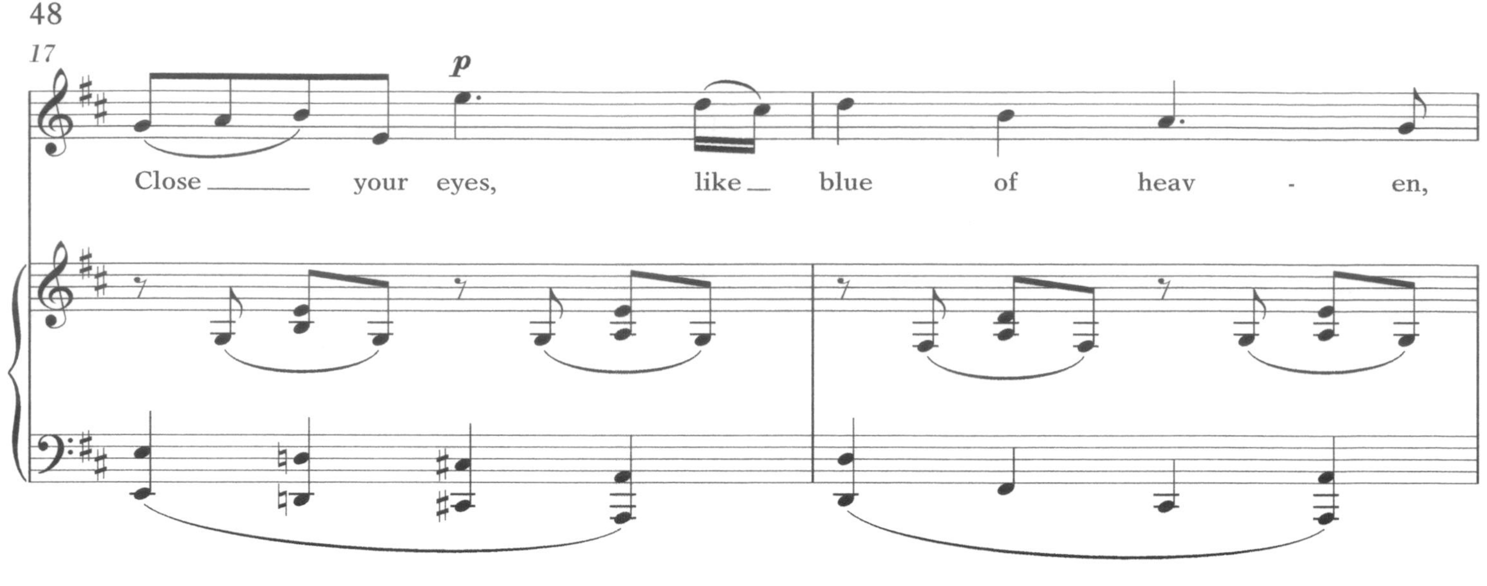
17
p
Close your eyes, like blue of heav - en,

19
rit.
a tempo
rit.
a tempo
rit.
Hush - a - bye, my dear! Bye, bye, bye,
a tempo
rit.
a tempo
rit.
rit.
p

22
a tempo
rall.
bye!
ten.
L.H.
pp a tempo
morendo
rall.
ppp

THIS LITTLE ROSE

Emily Dickinson*

William Roy

* Poem copyright, 1945, by Millicent Todd Bingham.

13
slightly accelerated
mp
17
p
On-ly a bee will miss it, On-ly a but - ter - fly,
p
21
Hast-en-ing from far jour - ney On _ its breast to lie.
25
slightly accelerated
mp cresc.

29
slightly accelerated
mf
a tempo
mf
On-ly a bird will
33
won - der,
On-ly a breeze will sigh,
sensitively
Ah, lit-tle rose, how
37
mp
rit.
p a tempo
eas - y For such as thee to die!
slightly
41
accelerated
p
mp

RIBBON BOW

John Jacob Niles

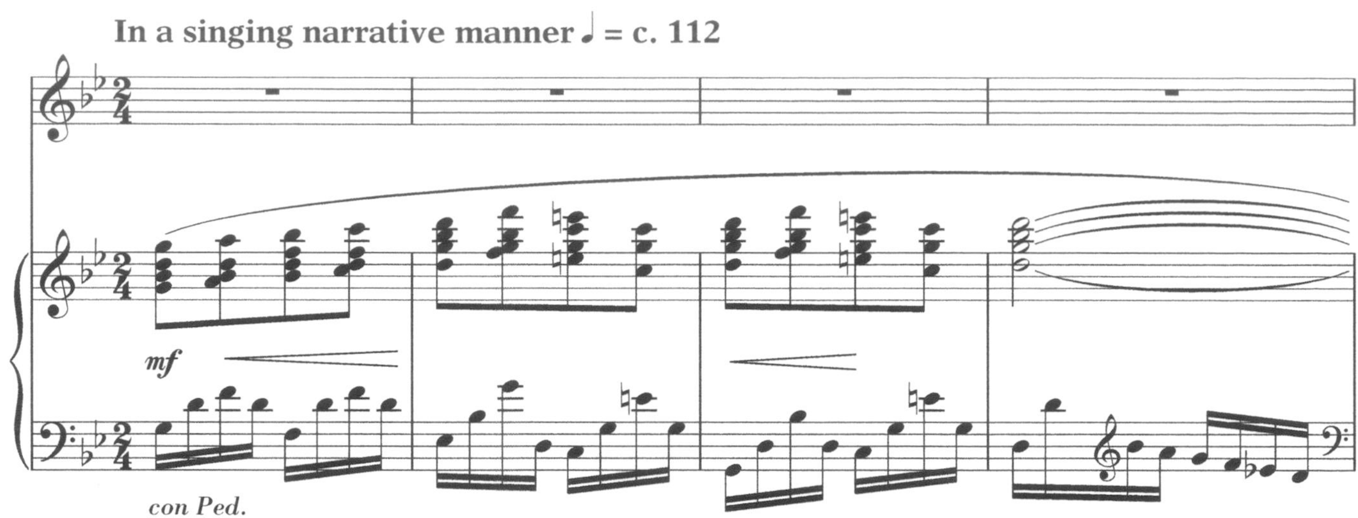

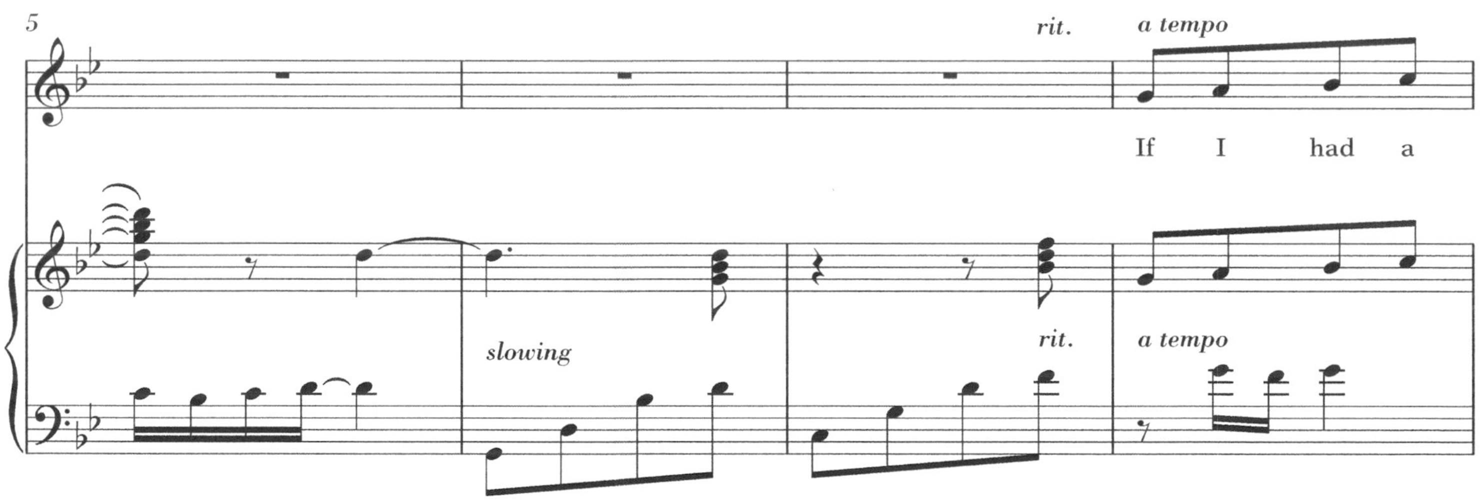

13
fan - cy sash, my own true love would think me fair. And
17
slower
when he goes to Frank - fort Log - gin' on the rise, He'd bring me back with his own hands A
slower
20
a tempo
ver - y pret - ty prize. If I had a rib - bon bow to bind my hair,
a tempo
p
24
If I had a fan - cy sash, my own true love would

28
rit.
think me fair.
rit.
33
a tempo
If I was like the cit - y brung and
a tempo
36
fair with smart,
Ne'er a lad in
39
all them parts would know my heart.

42
slower
Then I'd live in Frank-fort Where all the law-in' goes. I'd lark a-bout the set-tle-ments And
slower
45
a tempo
wear them furr-in' clothes. If I was like the cit-y brung and
a tempo
48
fair with smart,
Ne'er a lad in all them parts would
52
faster
know my heart.
faster

THE STATUE AT CZARSKOE-SELO

from *25 Poems by Pushkin*

Alexander Pushkin*

César Cui
Op. 57, No. 17

* English words based on the version by Charles Fonteyn Manney, Copyright, 1929, by Oliver Ditson Company.

21
a tempo
mf
O won - der! From the jar at her feet Flows a
a tempo
p
26
delay slightly
f
mar - vel - ous ra - diant foun - tain! Hope - less the
colla voce
mf
31
ritenuto
maid - en still sor - rows O'er end - less wa -
ritenuto
p
36
a tempo
p
rit. al fine
ters that flow.
a tempo
rit. al fine
8va
p
pp

to G. S. Aunt Bess

THY LOVE

Elizabeth Barrett Browning

Samuel Barber

Barber indicated no tempo or dynamics in his manuscript.

10
these things, in them-selves, be-lov'd may Be changed, or changed_ for
[♭]
13
thee; But love me for love's sake That ev-er-more,_
[𝄐]
16
Much slower
Thou mayst love on_ Thou mayst love on_
18
rit.
_ Through loves e-tern - i - ty.
rit.

YOUNG LOVE LIES SLEEPING

Christina Rossetti

Arthur Somervell

11
White lambs come graz - ing, White doves come
14
pp
build - ing there; And round a - bout him The
pp
17
May bush - es are white.
21
pp
Young Love lies dream - ing; But who can tell the
3
pp

24
dream? A per - fect sun - light On
27
rust - ling for - est tips, Or per - fect
30
moon - light Up - on a rip - pling stream; Or
pp
pp
33
per - fect si - lence, Or song of cher - ished lips.

37
mf
Draw close the cur - tains Of branch - ed
mf
40
e - ver - green; Change can - not touch them With
43
pp
fa - ded fin - gers sere
pp
47
Here the first vi - o - lets, Per -

50
haps will bud un-seen, And a dove
53
may-be Re-turn to nes-tle here. Young Love lies
f
f
57
sleep - ing, And round a-
p
61
bout him The May bush-es are white.
rit.
rit.
pp